MW00387267

THE 88 ESSENTIALS YOU MUST KNOW TO READ AND UNDERSTAND PROFIT & LOSS STATEMENTS AND KPI

Bernard FEVRY

mycampusfinance@gmail.com

1

CONTENTS

To the reader,

The profit and loss statement, called in US income statement, seems easy to read and understand and looks familiar.
However, it's necessary to go further to reveal the secrets of company's performance.

So, we analyze the components of the profit and loss statement to identify the key elements leading to the recurring performance of the company.
But the performance of a company should be analyze in terms of financial resources invested and financial needs employed.
That's why, it's necessary to review the components of the balance sheet reviewed as a financing system.

Then, the structure of the key performance indicators is used to build a chain of drivers and highlight the levers.

These steps are required for the creation of a company's private block chain for a financial forecast process and a budget control.

You are a shareholder and you want to read and understand the financial statements and especially the profit and loss statement provided by your company.

You are an entrepreneur and you want to better understand how the profit is generated by your business.

You are a banker and you want to read and understand the financial statements of your clients.

You are a student in a MBA or EMBA program and you would like to review quickly the information released by a profit and loss statement.

This book is for you

In few hours, you will assimilate the most important concepts to read and understand a profit and loss statement even if consolidated.

The book will provide to you some training exercises to test your new knowledge

It will open to you the access to the fantastic language of accounting and finance

You want to go further in accounting and finance?

Many other e-books and online courses are available in these topics

Please have a look at page 86 to discover our other books and our web site: mycampusfinance.com

WHY INCOME IS NOT CASH FLOW?

1 The profit and loss statement (also called income statement in US) calculates the profit after tax during a period (generally 12 months) called accounting period.

2 The concept of profit is sometimes confused with the concept of cash flow while they are different

3 The cash flow is the flow of cash (positive and negative) generated by the current and non recurrent activity of a company

4 The income (profit or loss) is the consequence of a calculation by difference between the revenues realized by a company and the costs incurred.
This way to recognize the revenues and the costs is called accrual accounting.

5 The relationship between the cash flow and the result is detailed in our book "The 88 essentials to read and understand a cash flow statement" published by AMAZON.

6 In some countries, very small companies are allowed to calculate their profit by difference between the revenues collected and the costs paid.
This method, called cash accounting, is less accurate to analyze the performance of a company.

But the cash situation is also important to be known, that's why companies record their inflows and outflows in another statement called "cash flow statement".

THE FINANCIAL STATEMENTS AND THEIR LINKS

7 Let's start with the balance sheet.
(The balance sheet is explained in details in our book published by AMAZON: "the 88 essentials you must know to read and understand a balance sheet").

The balance sheet shows a financial situation at a given date (called the closing date). This date is the last day of a period of 12 months called: "accounting period" or sometimes "accounting year".

8The balance sheet lists and values the assets and the liabilities of a company.
The balance between assets and liabilities is also the value of the company at the closing date given by the accounting books.
That's why, this value is called: "book value".
It is depicted as "Equity" in the balance sheet.

9 The income (profit or loss) is the variance of the book value (Equity) generated by the activity of the company between 2 closing dates so over a period of 12 months.
Because the company belongs to its shareholders, the variance of its book value is also the variance of the wealth of its shareholders.
So, the income can be analyzed as the variance of the wealth of its shareholders generated by the activity of their company between 2 closing dates

10 During the annual shareholders' meeting held after the closing date, the shareholders have to decide the allocation of the income:

- Distributed to shareholders as dividends in proportion of their stake in the company
- Retained in the company as reinvested capital (called retained earnings)

11 The balance sheet is also the list of the financial resources and needs of the company valued and balanced by the cash available (called net cash position) at the closing date.

12 The cash flow could be defined by the variance of the net cash position between 2 closing dates

13 We can say that the balance sheet, the profit and loss statement and the cash flow statement show the 3 dimensions of the financial situation of a company:

Its value: the balance sheet
Its performance: the profit and loss statement
Its cash variance: the cash flow statement

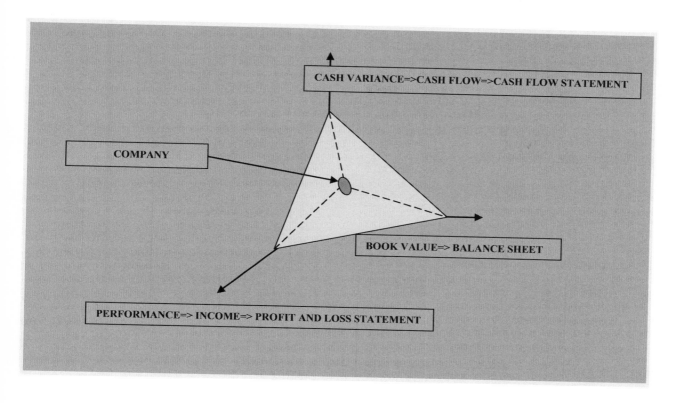

14 The 3 statements are linked together:

The variance of the equity between 2 closing dates is the result (profit or loss) and is depicted in the profit and loss statement while the variance of the net cash position is depicted in the cash flow statement.

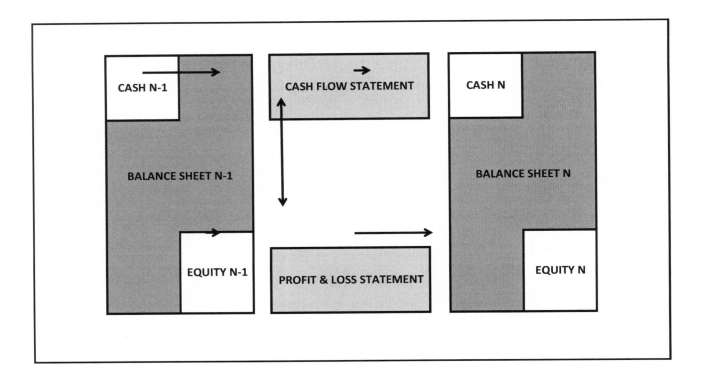

15 There is a 4th statement: the statement of retained earnings (sometimes called: statement of shareholders' equity). It analyzes in details the income allocation decided by the shareholders 'meeting and the non recurring variances of equity like issue of new shares.

We will review now the main points of the balance sheet necessary to understand the profit and loss statement and to calculate some key performance indicators.

REVIEW OF THE BALANCE SHEET

16 The accountants build a chart showing and valuing which belongs to the company and which is owed by the company.

17 Which belongs to the company is called "asset"
Which is owed by the company is called "liabilities".

The capital invested by the shareholders (called "Equity") is a debt, but a remarkable one, that's why we identify it from the other debts (due to suppliers, bankers and so an) called "liabilities".

18 The capital invested by the shareholders is also the value of the company (called "book value")

We can say that the value of a company has a double aspect:

The value of a company is the balance between which belongs to the company and which is owed by the company

Value of the company = Assets – Liabilities

And also:

Value of the company = the Invested Capital by shareholders (Equity)

The Invested Capital includes:

→ the capital invested from the beginning: "Capital" in UK or "Common Stock" in US
→ the profits of the last years not yet distributed as dividends: "Retained earnings"
→ the Result of the current year if it has not yet be allocated by the shareholders' meeting)

So we write:

Assets – Liabilities = Capital + Retained earnings + Result

Assets = Liabilities + Capital + Retained earnings + Result

19 The chart showing and valuing the assets on one side and the liabilities + Capital + Retained earnings + Result on the opposite side is called the "balance sheet".

By definition, the balance sheet is always balanced since it represents an equation

20 The sum of Capital + Retained earnings + Result is called "Equity".
So we can show the balance sheet with 2 sides:
One side represents the assets
The second side is includes "Liabilities + Equity".

The 2 sides are balanced and we write:

$$ASSETS = LIABILITIES + EQUITY$$

21 As we have seen in section 10: the result belongs to its owners (shareholders), so a meeting should be held every year to decide at the majority what to do with the result.

Two options are possible:
The profit can be distributed to the shareholders (dividends) or reinvested in the Company (retained earnings).
In fact, the decision is often in between.
A portion of profit is allocated to the shareholders as a return on their investments and the remaining is kept inside the company for further developments.

Consequently, the balance sheet at the closing date could be shown:

- before decision of the shareholders annual meeting with the identification of the result not yet allocated
- after decision of the shareholders annual meeting and so after allocation of the last result in dividends payable and addition to retained earnings

22 Never forget that the profit is an increase of the value of the company but not necessary a correlated increase of the cash available.

Indeed, the cash generated everyday by the performance could be already invested in assets or used to pay liabilities.

That's why sometimes the company cannot distribute all the recorded profit in cash dividends.

As we have explained in section 12, the result is not a cash flow

23 The cash flow is the variance of the net cash position.

The cash flow is the money flowing inside a company during a period coming from the revenues collected in cash and the expenditures paid by the company.
If the money collected is bigger than the money paid during a period, we say that the cash flow is positive; if lower the cash flow is negative.

The net cash position is the amount of money available at a given date.
The net cash position is the balance between the cash on hand, on bank accounts or invested on a short term basis (short term investments at low risk and easy tradable securities, fixed short term deposits) minus the cash borrowed through short term note payable and overdrafts.

The net cash position is a relative number:
Its sign is positive when the cash available and invested is bigger that the cash borrowed on a short term basis.
If not, its sign is negative.

We can say that the total cash flow during a period is defined by the balance between the net cash position at the end of the period and the net cash position at the beginning.

24 Let's analyze now the shape of a balance sheet:

We have usually two types of presentation:

The running format or report format: the assets section is shown at the top and the liabilities and equity section are presented below.

The account format: the balance sheet has two sides and figures the accounting equation: Assets = Liabilities + Equity.
The assets are listed and valued on the right hand side whereas the liabilities and equity are listed and valued on the right hand side.

Here you have an example of the account format

BALANCE SHEET as of …/…/…

ASSETS		LIABILITIES AND EQUITY	

CURRENT ASSETS
 Cash and cash equivalents
 Marketable securities
 Accounts receivable less allowance for
     doubtful accounts
 Inventories
 Prepaid expenses
 	
 TOTAL CURRENT ASSETS
 	
 FIXED ASSETS
 Tangible assets less
     accumulated depreciation
 Intangible assets
 Investments
 	
 TOTAL FIXED ASSETS
 	
 TOTAL ASSETS
		SHORT TERM LIABILITIES
		 Notes payable and bank overdrafts
		 Accounts payable
		 Other payable
		
		 TOTAL SHORT TERM LIABILITIES
		
		 LONG TERM LIABILITIES
		 Bonds
		 Long term bank loans
		
		 TOTAL LONG TERM LIABILITIES
		
		 EQUITY
		 Capital
		 Retained earnings
		
		 TOTAL EQUITY
		
		 TOTAL LIABILITIES AND EQUITY	

25 look at the assets:

That's the framework given by the US-GAAP (Generally Accepted Accounting Principles in US).

Note that another presentation according to IFRS (International Financial Reporting Standards) the assets are shown from the least liquid at the top (fixed assets usually called non-current assets like land and building) to the most liquid i.e. cash in current assets.

So under US-GAAP, the <u>current assets</u> are shown first.

The different listed items are cash and other assets expected to be converted into cash in less than one year:

-Cash and cash equivalent:
The amount of cash in hand, petty cash or in banking accounts.
The cash equivalent is less liquid and refers to very short term investments (less than 90 days) with a low risk
-Marketable securities:
The marketable securities are less liquid than cash equivalent with a longer maturity but shorter than one year.
-Accounts receivable:
This current asset refers to the outstanding bills for sales or services already provided by a company but not yet paid by the customers.
According to the conservatism principle seen further in section 30, an estimate should be made for the amount that is unlikely to be collected.
Because, it is only at this stage a potential loss, it is deducted in the balance sheet under the item:"allowance for doubtful accounts".
This allowance is adjusted later to the actual payment.
-Inventories:
Value of merchandise ready for sale in retail companies
Value of finished goods and also raw materials and work in progress not yet converted into finished goods in manufacturing companies.
The method of valuing refers always to the cost for the company, never to the expected selling price.
-Prepaid expenses:
A prepaid expense is an expenditure paid in one accounting period for an asset or a service consumed in a later accounting period.

Then in US-GAAP, we have the <u>fixed assets</u> (called non-current assets in IFRS)

They are supposed to be used during more than one year.

We have:

-Tangible assets sometimes named as Land and **P**roperty **P**lant and **E**quipment (**PPE**):
These fixed assets are physical assets like equipment, machinery, furniture, computers….
They are recorded at their purchase cost but adjusted every accounting cycle according to their use through the process of depreciation.
-Intangible assets:
By opposition with the tangible assets, the intangible assets are non physical like patents, copyrights, trade-marks, licenses, franchises…
They are recorded also at their purchase cost but adjusted through the process of impairment.
-Investments:
Investments are financial assets like stocks, bonds kept by the company during more than one year.

26 Look now at the right hand side: first the liabilities

Under US-GAAP, the <u>short term liabilities</u> (called current liabilities in IFRS) are shown first.

In short term liabilities, we list and value the debts incurred by the company due in less than one year:

17

-Note payable and bank overdraft:
Financial debt instrument created by formal legal documents e.g. promissory notes or credit granted by a bank during a short period of time and up to a maximum of amount.
-Accounts payable:
Accounts payable represent the total of invoices from the suppliers for the purchase of goods and services already received and not yet paid. It is a form of credit allowed by suppliers.
-Other payable:
Other payable refers to payable due to other creditors than suppliers like employees (salaries), government (taxes), stockholders (dividends)...

Then we have the <u>long term liabilities</u> (called non-current liabilities in IFRS).

They are mainly financial debt due in more than one year like:

-Bonds:
Financial instrument issued by the Company in order to raise money, which can be assimilated to a loan borrowed from public.
-Long term bank loans:
The list includes also long term leases that have been capitalized. The portion of long term liabilities (called current portion) is categorized as a short term liability.

27 At last we have the <u>equity</u>:

The owner's equity (single ownership company) or shareholders' equity is the net worth of the company given by difference between assets and liabilities but also the invested and reinvested capital by shareholders:
-The invested capital
 Given by the capital called Common stock in US.

-The reinvested capital
Called retained earnings in US, the reinvested capital is the portion of profit of the last years decided by shareholders to be kept inside the company (so reinvested) and not paid as dividends.

28 If we consider that accounting looks like a language useful to depict the financial situation of a company, the accounting principles can be assimilated to the grammar rules necessary to speak a correct language.
Governing the balance sheet, 2 main accounting principles are used:

Historical cost principle
Conservatism principle

29 Historical cost principle:

According to the historical principle, assets and liabilities are valued at their cost when entering in the patrimony of a company as assets or incurring as a liability

This principle looks relevant because accounting reports past events and requires consistency and comparability

30 Conservatism principle:

In the conservatism principle (also called prudence principle), we recognize a loss on an asset or a liability even if there is an uncertainty about the outcome when profit is only recognized when it is assured of being received.

This principle drives the impairment process in which any potential loss of assets or liabilities leads to a provision called "allowance".
2 types of assets are especially concerned: the inventories and the customers' receivable.

THE BALANCE SHEET: TRAINING EXERCISE

31 This is the balance sheet of "marvellous shoes", a US wholesale store selling shoes to retailers.

The figures are in thousand of US dollars.

The closing date is December 31st of the last calendar year called N-1

BALANCE SHEET as of 31/12/N-1 in 000 of $

ASSETS			LIABILITIES AND EQUITY	
CURRENT ASSETS			**SHORT TERM LIABILITIES**	
Cash and cash equivalents		148	Notes payable and bank overdrafts	290
Marketable securities			Accounts payable	109
Accounts receivable	283		Other payable	0
less allowance for doubtful accounts	0	283		
Inventories		322	**TOTAL SHORT TERM LIABILITIES**	399
Prepaid expenses		10		
			LONG TERM LIABILITIES	
TOTAL CURRENT ASSETS		763	Bonds	
			Long term bank loans	150
FIXED ASSETS				
Tangible assets	578		**TOTAL LONG TERM LIABILITIES**	150
less accumulated depreciation	229	349		
Intangible assets			**EQUITY**	
Investments		111	Capital	517
			Retained earnings	157
TOTAL FIXED ASSETS		460		
			TOTAL EQUITY	674
TOTAL ASSETS		1 223	**TOTAL LIABILITIES AND EQUITY**	1 223

32

Let's review the items:

We notice that the company has:

-Some cash available in bank accounts (cash = 148)
-An amount of 283 not yet collected from its customers (retailers) but no allowance for doubtful accounts
-A merchandise inventory (shoes) valued at 322
-Some prepaid expenses for 10 (rent paid in advance)
-Tangible assets (storage warehouses) for an historical value of 578 and depreciated of 229 to get a net value of 349
- An investment of 111 (value of shares owned) which is a stake in a shoes manufacturer

For the right hand side of the balance sheet, we have:
-An overdraft (note payable and overdraft = 290)
-Some accounts payable (109) due to suppliers
-Other payable (0) due to tax administration (income tax), shareholders (dividends), and employees (salaries of December) etc...
-A long term bank loan of 150
-A capital of 517 (517,000 shares of a nominal value of 1 $) which is the capital invested by the shareholders at the beginning of the business
-Retained earnings for 157 which are the profit of the last years that the shareholders have decided to keep within the Company instead of distributing as dividends. It looks like a reinvested capital.

This information is extracted from "the notes to financial statements" provided by the Company to explain some items.

PRESENTATION OF THE FINANCING SYSTEM

33 As we have seen: the balance sheet shows the assets and the liabilities of a company at a given date.

Now, we will transform it into a financing system showing the financial resources and the financial needs of a company at a given date.

34 We have depicted the 5 sections of the balance sheet provided by the accountant:

The fixed assets (non-current assets)
The current assets
The short term liabilities (current liabilities)
The long term liabilities (non-current liabilities)
The equity

But the balance sheet reveals also the financial position of the company called net cash position.

The net cash position computes the amount of cash available or invested on a short term basis and easily convertible into cash without any risk or with a slight risk.

This net cash position is in fact the balance between the financial long term resources raised and the financial needs.

So we need to identify the financial resources and financial needs and balance them with the net cash position.

35 Identification of 5 financial sections

The balance sheet is converted into 5 financial sections:

Two financial needs:

-The financial needs to grow in the future and develop the business
-The financial needs to run the day to day business

Two long term financial resources:

-The capital borrowed by the company
-The capital invested by shareholders or owners

The net cash position:

-The balance between long term financial resources and financial requirements.

Net cash position = long term financial resources – financial needs

If the net cash position is positive we have a liquid asset, if the net cash position is negative we have a short term financial liability.

What are the long term resources of financing?

36 The funds from lenders

These funds are coming mainly from bankers but people or companies can also lend money to big companies directly or through securities called bonds quoted in a bond market.

The funds should be repaid to the lenders after a fixed period of time (called maturity) and generate a reward called interest (fixed or variable).

The interest paid by the company is deductible from its income tax.

37 The funds from investors

The shareholders (sometimes a single owner) invest money in their company and get in exchange certificates of ownership called "shares".
The shares give them the right to make important decisions during the extraordinary shareholders' meetings (the run of the company is the job of the board of directors and executive management) and to decide the allocation of the yearly income during the annual shareholders' meetings.

What are the financial needs?

38 First the financial needs to grow in the future and develop the business

The fixed assets are defined to be used over than one year in order to participate to the development of the company in the future.
But since they must exist from now; they must be financed right now even if the return (earnings) will appear after some years.

39 Then the financial needs to run the day to day business

Since often sales are not collected cash but later;
Since in some activities, goods in inventories are needed to be shown to potential customers and ready to be delivered;
Since, a company get some credit from its suppliers;

The cash missing because some inventories are not yet sold, some sales are not yet collected even if some expenses are paid later on credit is called: **WCR**: **W**orking **C**apital **R**equirement

A company needs to finance this working capital requirement as it has to finance the fixed assets invested to grow in the future.

40 The net cash position

Calculated as a balance between long term resources of funds and funds requirements:

Net cash position = funds from lenders + funds from investors – funds required to develop the company (fixed assets) – funds necessary to run the company (working capital requirement)

41 Calculation of the WCR

We have define in section 39 the WCR as the amount of money needed to run the day to day business

We calculate by adding the missing cash not yet recovered from the inventories and the receivables and deducting the extra cash because some payable are not yet paid

The formula is:

WCR = inventories + accounts receivable + other receivable – accounts payable – other payable

As you can see, the WCR **never** includes the cash available (cash and cash equivalent, marketable securities) and the short term financial liabilities (note payable and overdraft).

Usually, to focus only on the business cycle, we compute the operating WCR as:

Inventories + accounts receivable – accounts payable

The other receivable and other payable are often either non-recurring or items that we cannot easily manage or intervene like credit tax, tax payable and salaries payable etc...

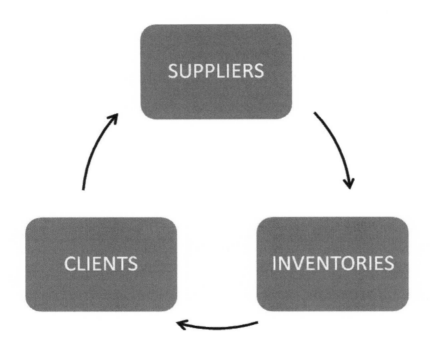

So if a company is stable in its operating management (inventories turnover, collection of receivable and payment of payable) the operating WCR is proportional to the sales of the company which means that doubling sales will double the operating WCR.

<u>Pay attention</u>: The WCR could be negative if the payable (accounts and other) are bigger than the sum of inventories, receivable (accounts and other) and prepaid expenses.

Then, the WCR is not a need but a resource of cash.

We could find this situation if a company had a very high turnover of inventories (or no inventories at all because it provides services), makes cash sales and delays the payment of its suppliers.

So the sign of the WCR and its amplitude depend on the type of business of the company i.e. the WCR of a business jets dealer is very different to the WCR of a supermarket.

42 Now we can build the financing system of a company

As defined by Oxford Dictionaries, a system is "a set of things working together as parts of a mechanism or an interconnecting network or a set of principles or procedures according to which something is done".

We have defined above the financial resources and needs; we will highlight them from the assets and the liabilities of the balance sheet.

Some transformations are necessary to build our financing system:

First, we directly identify the equity and the long term liabilities (long term debt) as financial resources and the fixed assets as financial needs.

Then, we have to calculate another financial need: the working capital requirement (WCR)

Working capital requirement = Inventories + accounts receivable + other receivable – accounts payable – other payable

At last, we compute the net cash position:

Net cash position = cash + marketable securities + fixed short term deposits – note payable – current portion of long term liabilities.

So, we have 5 items

The first 3 items are always positive or equal to 0 (except rarely for equity in case of important cumulative losses) and will be located on the same side that the balance sheet in the account format:

-   Fixed assets on the left hand side of the system

-   -Equity and long term liabilities on the right hand side of the system

For the last 2 items: Working capital requirement and Net cash position, their sign is either positive or negative.

If the item is positive, it is located on the left hand side of the system
If the item is negative, it is located on the right hand side of the system

A last check is very important: our system should have 2 balanced sides (if not, it means that one item in the balance sheet item has not been correctly reported at its right location in the financing system)

Finally, we calculate and draw every item of the system in percentage of the total of each side.

This framework is named common size financing system

Common size: because the 5 items are proportionally calculated and represented.
Financing: because we have financing resources facing financial needs and the balance is coming from the net cash position.

43 Representation of the common size financing system

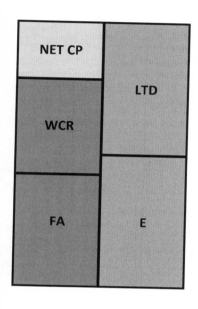

Look at this representation of the common size financing system.

Equity (**E**) and long term debt or (**LTD**) are in green and show the long term financial resources.
Fixed assets (**FA**) and working capital requirement (**WCR**) are in blue and show the financial needs.

The net cash position (**NET CP**) is in yellow and balances the system.

The systems are built from balance sheets set at the closing date. In most cases, the closing date is December 31st, last day of the calendar year, but according to the seasonality of their business or specific rules like in Japan, companies choose an accounting cycle different from the calendar year.

According to the signs and the proportions of the items, we can define eight remarkable financing systems.

You are invited to refer to our book published by AMAZON "the 88 essentials you must know to read and understand a balance sheet". You will learn about the strengths and weaknesses of every financing system, their risks and the ways to face them.

The common size financing system of "marvellous shoes" is calculated and analyzed in section 78.

It will be used to assess the performance of the company after building its key performance indicators (KPI).

So, after these preliminary explanations, it's time to come back to the profit and loss statement.

THE PROFIT & LOSS STATEMENT

44 As we did in section 28 for the balance sheet, it's important to know the "grammar rules", I mean the main accounting principles used to build a profit and loss statement:

The net income (profit or loss) is the balance between the revenues earned (collected in cash or not yet) and the costs incurred (already paid or not yet) to provide these revenues.

This definition is summarized under the concept called "accrual accounting" (refer to section 4 to 6)

So, the main accounting principles are used to define how the revenues and expenses are recorded to calculate the net income:

The realization principle will define the revenues earned

The matching principle will define the costs incurred

45 Realization principle

Revenues are income expressed in monetary terms gained by an entity from its business activity usually from the sale of goods and services to customers

We consider that revenues are earned in a period if the good sold is delivered or if the service is performed in whole or substantially during the period

We say that the revenue is recognized or realized in the period

An expense is an outcome spent to acquire an item or a service.

We classify the expenses into operating expenses (like the cost of labor and materials expended to create products), financial expenses arising from the borrowing of money (like the interest expense), capital expenses (expenditures) to generate income over multiple periods (like the purchase of a building)

We consider that an expense is consumed in a period if either the expense occurs to produce a revenue earned in a period (product expense like the cost of goods sold) or occurs in the period (period expense like the rent expense, the insurance expense or the interest expense)

For capital expenses likely generating revenues over multiple periods, we don't record its monetary value (for example the purchase price of an equipment) to calculate the profit during the period but the cost of use of the equipment during the period
This cost is called the depreciation expense of the equipment in the period

To summarize, the profit or the loss of an entity during a period is calculated as the balance between the revenues realized during the period and the expenses occurred (consumed) during the same period.

The expenses of a period should be matched with the revenues during the same period.

47 The net income is a measure of the performance of a company during a period balancing recorded revenues and expenses in the period to which they relate.

Revenues increase the value of the company (equity) and expenses reduce the equity that's why the variance of equity showed in the balance sheet is also the balance between the revenues and the expenses.

In other words the profit or loss showed by the balance sheet is also the profit or loss given by the profit and loss statement.

48 The profit and loss statement: a five-stage rocket

The profit and loss statement shows the net income through a multiple steps calculation.

Starting from the net sales and services realized (net means here after commercial discounts given to clients), we define 5 steps to calculate the net income:

- ✓ The gross profit: profit realized after deducting the costs directly associated (called cost of goods sold or cost of sales) to sell its products or to provide its services.
- ✓ The **E**arning **B**efore **I**nterest and **T**ax (EBIT): profit realized after deducting from the above gross profit **S**elling, **G**eneral and **A**dministrative expenses SGA (overheads and other indirect costs except non recurrent costs and gains, financial expenses and revenues and income tax).
The EBIT measures the profit generated by the company ignoring exceptional operations, tax burden, costs and revenues from the capital structure.

- ✓ The **E**arning **B**efore **T**ax (EBT): profit realized before calculation of the income tax
- ✓ The **N**et **I**ncome (NI): profit realized after calculation of the income tax
- ✓ The last step shows the allocation to retained earnings after deduction of dividends decided by the shareholders annual meeting.

49 This is the profit and loss statement of "marvellous shoes" for the present calendar year N.

PROFIT & LOSS STATEMENT in 000 of $	YEAR N
Net sales and services	2 211
- Cost of sales	1 599
Gross profit	612
- Selling, general and administrative expenses	402
Earnings before interest and tax*	210
+Non recurrent gains	10
- Interest expenses	69
+ Financial revenues	0
Earnings before tax	151
- Income tax	60
Net Income	91
- Dividends	38
Addition to Retained earnings	53
*depreciation expense included 100	

50 We recognize the starting point in green "Net sales and services" for 2,211,000 $.

Then we have the 5 steps of calculation in yellow.

The net income is calculated as 91,000 $.

The annual shareholders meeting has decided to distribute 38,000 $ as dividends so an amount of 53,000 $ is added to the retained earnings of the balance sheet end of year N.

The costs involved in the calculation of the EBIT are figured by destination (direct costs, selling costs…) and not by nature (salaries, depreciation expense etc…).

The amount of depreciation expense is notified by a * for an amount of 100,000 $ in order to calculate the EBITDA (**E**arnings **B**efore **I**nterest **T**ax **D**epreciation and **A**mortization).

The EBITDA is a very important concept that we develop in our book published by AMAZON "the 88 essentials you must know to read and understand a cash flow statement"

As we did for the balance sheet in sections 33 and following, we need to adapt the profit and loss statement and transform it into a performing system able to identify later the key performance indicators (KPI)

BUILDING THE PERFORMING SYSTEM

51 Everybody knows the Russian nesting dolls that fit into each other.

We have a similar concept with the profit and loss statement.

From the sales (the starting point), we select 3 steps among 5: the gross margin, the EBIT and the net income.

We start from the sales (and services) considered as the main source of revenues for a company.

We select the gross margin to have a first idea of the profitability of products and services.

We have the EBIT considered as the profit generated by the recurrent business of the company.

At last, we take the net income: the profit generated by recurrent, non recurrent and financial activities calculated after the income tax.

This profit belongs to the shareholders and could be distributed as dividends or reinvested in the company as addition to retained earnings.

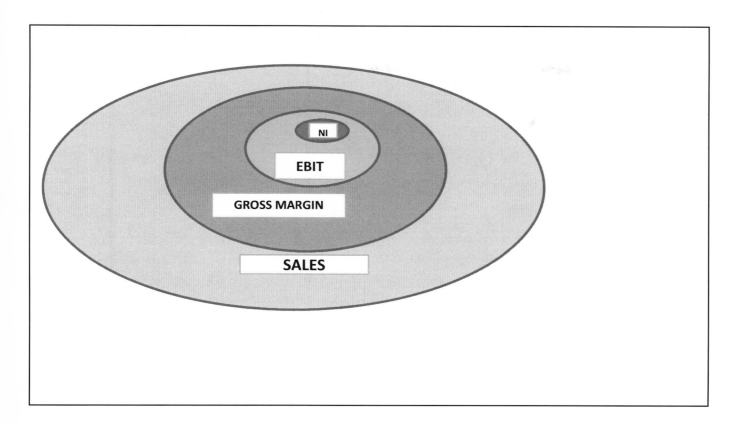

If we want to analyze the performance of the company and especially the recurrent performance of the business after tax, we need to recalculate the performance process by dissociating the performance issued by the recurrent operations, the performance issued by the non recurrent operations and the performance issued by the financial activities.

Every performance should be calculated after income tax.

52 In the chart below, we reprocess the data to increase the relevance of information.

We show in yellow the data directly given by the profit and loss statement: EBIT, net financial expenses (the balance between interest expenses and financial revenues), non recurrent items, net income and total income tax.

The income tax is calculated in the profit and loss statement just below the EBT (earnings before tax) but as it impacts every component (EBIT, net financial expenses and non recurrent items), we must calculate them after tax.

First we compute the income tax rate by dividing the income tax by the earnings before tax (EBT).

R_T = income tax/ EBT

This rate is sometimes called effective tax rate.

Then we calculate the impact of the income tax on the EBIT:

- Income tax on EBIT = EBIT* R_T (in light brown on the chart)
- EBIT after income tax = EBIT - EBIT* R_T = EBIT * (1- R_T)
- EBIT after income tax is called NOPAT: **N**et **O**perating **P**rofit **A**fter **T**ax (in dark brown on the chart)

Now, we calculate the impact of the income tax on the net financial expenses:

- Income tax on net **Financial EXP**enses = $FEXP \cdot R_T$ (in light blue on the chart)
- FEXP after income tax = $FEXP - FEXP \cdot R_T = FEXP \cdot (1 - R_T)$
- FEX after income tax is called FEXPAT = net **F**inancial **EXP**enses **A**fter **T**ax (in dark blue on the chart)

You notice that if we have more financial expenses than financial revenues, the balance is a net financial expense deductible of the taxable basis.
So, the impact of the income tax on the net financial expense is a tax saving.

At last, we calculate the impact of the income tax on the non recurrent gains or losses. (Non recurrent items):

- Income tax on **N**on **R**ecurrent **I**tems = $NRI \cdot R_T$ (in light grey on the chart)
- NRI after income tax = $NRI - NRI \cdot R_T = NRI \cdot (1 - R_T)$
- NRI after income tax is called NRIAT = **N**on **R**ecurrent **I**tems **A**fter **T**ax (in dark grey on the chart)

The **R**ecurrent **I**ncome **A**fter **T**ax (RIAT) in green in the chart is calculated as the balance between Net **O**perating **P**rofit **A**fter **T**ax (NOPAT) and the net **F**inancial **EXP**enses **A**fter **T**ax (FEXPAT)

We need now to make a double check of our calculations in the lower part of the chart:

➜ The net income is the sum of the RIAT and NRIAT
➜ The income tax is the sum of the income tax on EBIT and NRI minus the tax saving on the net financial expenses

39

NON REC ITEMS		Net Financial Expenses	
Inc tax/NRI	NRIAT	Tax saving	FEXPAT

Total Income Tax	Tax saving

Income Tax / EBIT	NOPAT

EBIT

Total Income Tax	NRIAT	RIAT

NET INCOME

53 Building the performing system to calculate ratios

At this stage, we are able to calculate some ratios in order to have a first idea of the performance of the company.

A ratio is an elegant way to calculate, track and compare data usually provided by financial statements.

A ratio is a quotient of 2 values to give a percentage allowing a follow-up over time within a company or a comparison between companies of different size providing financial statements in different currency.

Because the sales and services are the main source of revenue, we use them as a denominator of the quotient.

We propose 3 business performance ratios:

- The gross margin = gross profit / sales and services.
  To track and compare the margin of products sold and services provided and make "production or outsourcing" decisions

- The **N**et **O**perating **M**argin (NOM) = NOPAT/ sales and services.
  To track and compare the operating performance of the company

- The **R**eturn **O**n **S**ales (ROS) = RIAT / sales and services
  To track and compare the overall <u>recurrent</u> performance

In sections 65 and following, we will analyze, with the key performance indicators, how the business performance of a company leads to its efficiency performance and its financial performance.

By cracking the performance indicators, we will highlight their drivers.

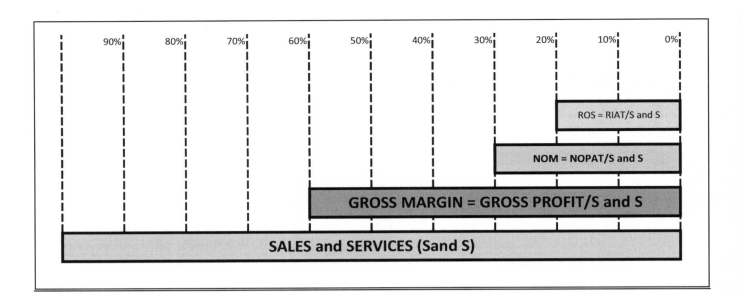

THE PERFORMING SYSTEM: TRAINING EXERCISE

54 Coming back to the profit and loss statement of the company "marvellous shoes" for the year N in thousands of dollars.

PROFIT & LOSS STATEMENT in 000 of $	YEAR N
Net sales and services	2 211
- Cost of sales	1 599
Gross profit	612
- Selling, general and administrative expenses	402
Earnings before interest and tax*	210
+Non recurrent gains	10
- Interest expenses	69
+ Financial revenues	0
Earnings before tax	151
- Income tax	60
Net Income	91
- Dividends	38
Addition to Retained earnings	53
*depreciation expense included 100	

We identify first the important data and then reprocess them to calculate the NOPAT, the FEXPAT and the NRIAT

At last, we calculate, the gross margin, the NOM and the ROS

43

We can find easily the 3 steps in the calculation of the profit:

- The gross profit = 612
- The EBIT = 210
- The net income = 91
-

All figures are in thousands of dollars and rounded.

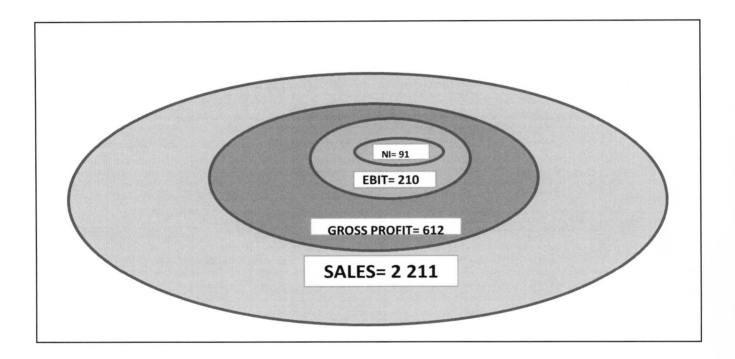

We show in yellow on the chart the data directly given by the profit and loss statement:

EBIT = 210

Net financial expenses (the balance between interest expenses and financial revenues) = 69 – 0 = 69

Non recurrent items = +10 (because it's a gain)

Net income = 91

Income tax = 60

First we compute the income tax rate by dividing the income tax by the earnings before tax (EBT).

R_T = income tax/ EBT = 60 / 151 = 39.7 %

Then we calculate the impact of the income tax on the EBIT:

- Income tax on EBIT = EBIT* R_T = 210 *39.7 % = 83 (in light brown on the chart)
- EBIT after income tax = EBIT * (1- R_T) = 210 * 60.3 % = 127
- EBIT after income tax =NOPAT = 127 (in dark brown on the chart)

Now, we calculate the impact of the income tax on the net financial expenses:

- Income tax on net **Financial EXP**enses = FEXP*R_T =69*39.7 % = 27 which is a tax saving (in light blue on the chart)
- FEXP after income tax = FEXP * (1- R_T) = 69 * 60.3 % = 42
- FEX after income tax = FEXPAT = 42 (in dark blue on the chart)

You notice that if we have more financial expenses than financial revenues, the balance is a net financial expense deductible of the taxable basis getting a tax saving.

45

At last, we calculate the impact of the income tax on the non recurrent gains or losses. (Non recurrent items):

- Income tax on **N**on **R**ecurrent **I**tems = $NRI*R_T$ = 10 *39.7% = 4 (in light grey on the chart)
- NRI after income tax = $NRI * (1- R_T)$ = 10 * 60.3 % = 6
- NRI after income tax = NRIAT = 6 (in dark grey on the chart)

The **R**ecurrent **I**ncome **A**fter **T**ax (RIAT) in green on the chart is calculated as the balance between the NOPAT and FEXPAT
RIAT = 127 – 42 = 85

We need now to make a double check of our calculations in the lower part of the chart:

→ The net income is the sum of the RIAT and NRIAT:
85 + 6 = 91
→ The income tax is the sum of the income tax on EBIT and NRI minus the tax saving on the net financial expenses:
60 = 83 + 4 – 27 = 60

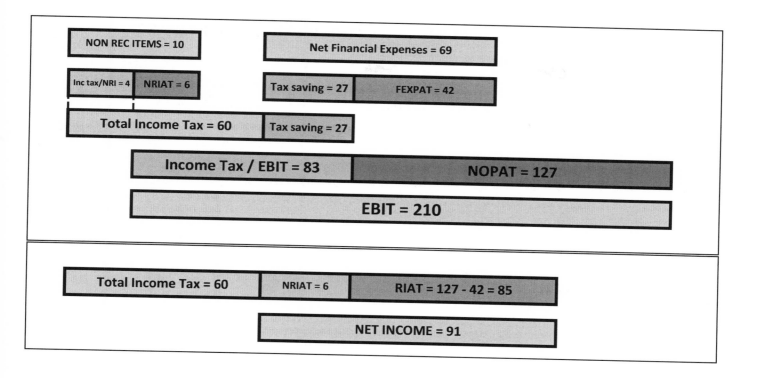

56 building the performing system

The amount of sales and services = 2 211

The 3 business performance ratios are:

- The gross margin = gross profit / sales and services.
  The gross margin = 612 / 2211 = 27.7 %

- The **N**et **O**perating **M**argin (NOM) = NOPAT/ sales and services.
  The NOM = 127 / 2211 = 5.7 %

- The **R**eturn **O**n **S**ales (ROS) = RIAT / sales and services
  The ROS = 85 / 2211 = 3.8 %

The above ratios should be calculated period by period within the company and compare with those of companies in the same type of industry

ROS = RIAT/SALES = 3,8 %

NOM = NOPAT/SALES = 5,7 %

GROSS MARGIN = GROSS PROFIT/SALES = 27,7 %

THE CONSOLIDATED PROFIT AND LOSS STATEMENT

57 Different types of techniques are used to combine 2 or more entities together.

1°) merger: a company acquires another company which ceases to exist and becomes part of the acquiring company.

2°) acquisition: the acquiring company (called parent or mother company) obtains control (full or partial) of the acquired company (the daughter company) but both companies keep their structure and are combined in a third entity called "group".

3°) consolidation: A new company is especially created to consolidate the assets, liabilities, revenues and costs of 2 companies.
Their shareholders receive in exchange common shares of the new company.
(On the contrary, a spinoff is the creation of an independent company from an existing business or division expecting that the new independent company will be more profitable than as a part of a larger business).

58 Control versus ownership

The ownership defines the level of stake a company (or a shareholder) has in another company.
The control means the aptitude to run and decide management and Board of Directors actions.
Theoretically, if the shareholders have the majority of votes, they can exercise the full control of the Company but practically this situation suffers many exceptions.

The consolidation process is a technique combining in a single financial statement all the financial statements of entities gathered in a group according the technique of acquisition seen in 2°) above.

In the consolidation process, we use the percentage of control and not the percentage of ownership.

59 The scope of consolidation

The scope of consolidation is the list of entities including:

- The parent company
- The companies hold directly or indirectly at the level of 20 % of control by the parent company

The statements of the companies inside the scope are aggregated with the statements of the parent Company according to methods explained further.

The companies outside the scope but hold by the parent company are represented in its balance sheet by the historical cost of acquisition in the non-current (fixed) assets section under the item investments and by dividends received in financial revenues of its income statement.

60 Methods of consolidation

Basically, there are 2 methods of consolidation:

-Full consolidation
-Equity consolidation

61 Full consolidation

This method is used when the parent Company has the full control of its daughter company.

The full control is supposed to exist if the mother company holds directly or indirectly at least 50 % of the control of its daughter. Then 100 % of costs and revenues of the daughter company are aggregated to its income statement (and 100 % of assets and liabilities are aggregated to the balance sheet of the mother company).

The difference of net profit (or loss) between the 100 % of aggregation and the real percentage of ownership of the mother company in its daughter is attributed to "minority interests".

Some adjustments are necessary: i.e. elimination of intra group transactions (sales and costs...), translation of foreign entities accounts in the currency of the parent company etc....

62 Equity consolidation

This method is used when the parent Company has a "significant influence" on its daughter company.

The significant influence is supposed to exist if the mother company holds directly or indirectly less than 50 % of the control of its daughter but more than 20 % to be in the scope of consolidation.

Then no costs and revenues of the daughter company are aggregated to the income statement of the mother company but the net profit (or loss) of the daughter company in proportion of the level of ownership is added to its result

CONSOLIDATION: TRAINING EXERCISE

63 We suppose a group in which the mother company has a percentage of control of 80 % in the daughter company D1 and 40 % in the daughter company D2.
If we consider the scope of consolidation, the group will include the mother company and the two daughters.
For the methods to be applied the daughter D1 is fully consolidated and the daughter D2 is equity consolidated.

64 Consolidated profit and loss statement of the group

Every consolidated item is the sum of 100 % of the corresponding item of the mother company + 100 % of the corresponding item of the daughter D1 (fully consolidated).

The items of D2 are ignored (equity consolidated)

For example: the consolidated sales are 1 100 = 100 + 1 000 because we ignore the sales of D2.

At last, we get a total net income of 322 (in blue) which is the sum of the net income of the mother company (42) and the net income of D1 (280).

But, because the mother company has only 80 % of D1 and 40 % of D2, the consolidated profit should be modified by deducting 20 % of the net income of D1 and adding 40 % of the net income of D2.

The consolidated profit is 322 – 20% * 280 + 40 % * 70 = 294

Double check: the consolidated profit is the profit of the mother company + 80 % of the profit of D1 + 40 % of the profit of D2.

The consolidation has no influence on the result of the group; it's only a way to show the items of the income statement under control.

CONSOLIDATED PROFIT & LOSS STATEMENT

	MOTHER	DAUGHTER 1 80%	DAUGHTER 2 40%	GROUP M+D1+D2
SALES	100	1 000	500	1 100
COST OF GOODS SOLD	20	400	200	420
GROSS PROFIT	80	600	300	680
SELLING/GENERAL/ADMINISTRATIVE	10	100	150	110
EBIT	70	500	150	570
INTEREST EXPENSE	10	100	50	110
EBT	60	400	100	460
INCOME TAX	18	120	30	138
TOTAL NET INCOME	42	280	70	322
-NET PROFIT TO MINORITY INTERESTS		280*20%		-56
+NET PROFIT FROM EQUITY CONSOLIDATEDCOMPANIES			70*40%	+28
NET PROFIT OF THE GROUP				294
		DOUBLE CHECK : 42 + 280*80% +70*40%		294

FROM PROFIT TO PERFORMANCE INDICATORS

65 The calculation of the net income (profit or loss) is important, but we have to integrate it in a synthesis of the performance of the company.

For that, the concept of "**K**ey **P**erformance **I**ndicators" (KPI) is very useful.

66 First we must review the concept of financing system seen in sections 33 and following.
(See more details in our book published by AMAZON: "the 88 essentials you must know to read and understand a balance sheet").

We have displayed the balance sheet as a system "financing system" showing the financial situation at the closing date.

Two financial needs are important: the fixed assets (**FA**) to develop the company in the future and the working capital requirement (**WCR**) if positive to run the business.
These needs are called "Capital Employed" (**CE**)

The funds financing the capital employed (**CE**) is coming from the investment of shareholders: equity (**E**) and the long term loans from lenders: long term debt (**LTD**).
The sum of equity (**E**) and long term debt (**LTD**) is called Invested Capital (**IC**)

The balance between the invested capital and the capital employed is the cash available called **N**et **C**ash **P**osition (**NCP**)

67 The common size financing system shows proportionally the capital employed and the invested capital.

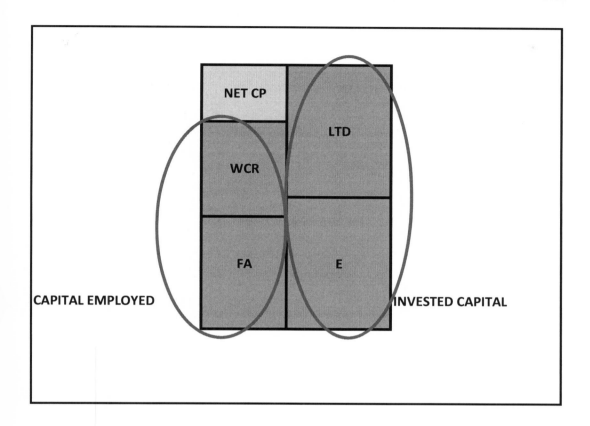

3 points have to be explained:

1°) if the working capital requirement (**WCR**) is negative; it becomes a financial resource so an invested capital instead of a capital employed.
 2°) the positive net cash position (**NET CP**) is never considered as capital employed but as a balance between invested capital and capital employed.
3°) if the net cash position (**NET CP**) is negative; it becomes also a financial resource (short term) so an invested capital

68 We define now 3 stages in the performance so 3 **Key Performance Indicators:**

- ✓ The business performance
- ✓ The efficiency performance
- ✓ The financial performance

69 The business performance analyzes the ability of the company to provide products and/or services at a cost lower than the selling price: independently of the non recurrent costs and gains and the capital structure revenues and expenses.

So, if you look at the framework of the income statement seen in sections 48 and following, we will use the Earning Before Interest and Tax (EBIT) calculated after the impact of the income tax.

If the average tax rate (effective tax rate) is T_R, computed as:

$$T_R = \frac{Income\ tax}{Earnings\ before\ tax}$$

The EBIT after tax is:

$$EBIT * (1 - T_R)$$

We call it **Net Operating Profit After Tax** = NOPAT

As we have seen in section 53, in order to compare it with the NOPAT of other companies, it is more efficient to calculate a percentage (a ratio) to get some relevant information comparable because independent from the currency and the size of the companies analyzed in the sample.

We will compare NOPAT to sales and services during the same period to get the **Net Operating Margin (NOM)**:

$$Net\ Operating\ Margin = \frac{NOPAT}{Sales}$$

This percentage will give a first idea of the profitability of the business developed by a company.

70 But the company needs also a structure of capital: the capital employed (**CE**) to develop and run the business.

We calculate the efficiency of the capital employed by defining the **Return On Capital Employed (ROCE)**

The ROCE is a quotient so a percentage which compares the NOPAT to the amount of Capital Employed (CE) to reach this NOPAT:

$$ROCE = \frac{NOPAT}{CE} = \frac{NOPAT}{FA + WCR}$$

So the ROCE looks like a return on the recurrent business through its capital employed.

Looking at the structure of the ROCE, three points should be highlighted:

- Any action to decrease a positive WCR will increase the efficiency of the company

- As seen in section 67, if the WCR is negative, it becomes an invested capital and not a capital employed so never use it in the calculation of the ROCE

- You could find in some books another way to calculate the ROCE:

$$ROCE = \frac{NOPAT}{E + net\ D}$$

→ E is the equity of the company
→ net D is the net debt of the company so its long term financial liabilities after deduction of the positive net cash position

But, if we look again at the common size financing system:

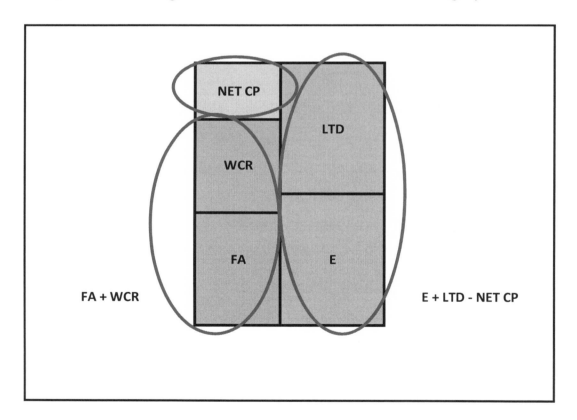

The balance of the system shows that:

$$FA + WCR = E + LTD - NET\ CP$$

LTD – NET CP is a net debt (**net D**) because it is the balance between the long term debt and the net cash position

We can write that $FA + WCR = E + net\ D$ so the 2 ways to calculate the ROCE are similar.

71 If we look now at the financial performance, the invested capital is the sum of equity and long term debt.(and the net position if negative)

The financial performance could be given by the return on the resources invested in the company (**E + LTD**).

But concerning the resources invested by the lenders (usually bankers), the return is easy to calculate since it is the interest rate of the long term debt paid by the company if the debt is repaid on time.

For the shareholders, the return is given by the recurrent income after financial expenses and revenues and of course after tax.

The capital invested from the beginning by the shareholders and supplemented later by the retained earnings is recorded in the equity.

So the return called "**Return On Equity**" (**ROE**) is defined as:

$$Return\ On\ Equity = \frac{RIAT}{Equity}$$

RIAT is the **Recurrent Income After Tax** seen and calculated in section 52

72 Cracking the performance indicators: the magic chain

A great advantage is to show the link between the business performance (NOM), the efficiency performance (ROCE) and the investment performance (ROE)

We use a formula in arithmetic of quotients which is:

$$\frac{A}{B} = \frac{A}{C} * \frac{C}{B}$$

(If B and C are $\neq 0$)

If A/B and A/C are 2 performance indicators, we have their link through C/B which is a driver.

From step to step, we can create a magic chain of drivers linking the performance indicators.
Some calculations are necessary but if you hate mathematics, you can skip the demonstration to reach directly the conclusions in section 74.

73 calculation of the magic chain

First, we calculate the link between return on equity (ROE) and return on capital employed (ROCE):

We start from the recurrent income after tax (RIAT) calculated in the income statement (See section 52)

$$RIAT = NOPAT - FEXPAT$$

The recurrent income after tax is the net operating profit after tax (NOPAT) less the net financial expenses after tax

So if:

$$\text{Return On Equity} = \frac{RIAT}{Equity}$$

We have:

$$ROE = \frac{NOPAT - FEXPAT}{Equity} = \frac{NOPAT}{Equity} - \frac{FEXPAT}{Equity}$$

Using the arithmetic of quotients:

$$\frac{NOPAT}{Equity} = \frac{NOPAT}{E + net\ D} * \frac{E + net\ D}{Equity}$$

$$\frac{FEXPAT}{Equity} = \frac{FEXPAT}{NOPAT} * \frac{NOPAT}{E + net\ D} * \frac{E + net\ D}{Equity}$$

So at last:

$$ROE = \frac{NOPAT}{E + net\ D} * \frac{E + net\ D}{Equity} - \frac{FEXPAT}{NOPAT} * \frac{NOPAT}{E + net\ D} * \frac{E + net\ D}{Equity}$$

E = equity and net D = net financial debt which is the balance between the financial debt and the cash available

We recognize the definition of return on capital employed (ROCE) used in section 70

$$ROCE = \frac{NOPAT}{E + net\ D}$$

Applying also the rule for quotients that:

$$(A + B)/ A = A/A + A/B = 1 + A/B$$

We have:

$$\frac{E + net\ D}{Equity} = 1 + \frac{net\ D}{Equity} = 1 + \frac{net\ D}{E}$$

So:

$$ROE = ROCE * \left(1 + \frac{net\ D}{E}\right) - \frac{FEXPAT}{NOPAT} * ROCE * \left(1 + \frac{net\ D}{E}\right)$$

Now, we introduce:

$$\varphi = \frac{FEXPAT}{NOPAT}$$

φ is the burden of the financial expenses compared to the operating profit but also the inverse of the well known ratio TIE (**T**imes **I**nterest **E**arned).

We get by factoring ROCE and 1 + (net D/E):

$$ROE = ROCE * \left(1 + \frac{net\ D}{E}\right) * (1 - \varphi)$$

This equation shows the link between 2 performance indicators: ROE and ROCE through 2 drivers: 1 + (net D)/E and (1-φ).

Last point: we define the relationship between return on capital employed (ROCE) and net operating margin (NOM)

$$ROCE = \frac{NOPAT}{SALES} * \frac{SALES}{FA + WCR}$$

We recognize NOPAT/SALES as the business performance indicator called NOM (**N**et **O**perating **M**argin)

SALES/ (FA + WCR) is a driver called **Capital Turnover (CT)** showing the level of sales reached with a given level of capital employed.

$$ROCE = NOM * CT$$

At last (whew!!) the link between the financial performance (ROE) and the business performance (NOM) is:

$$ROE = NOM * CT * \left(1 + \frac{net\ D}{E}\right) * (1 - \varphi)$$

63

74 Explanation of the magic chain

We have calculated in section 73 above that:

$$ROCE = NOM * CT$$

$$ROE = ROCE * \left(1 + \frac{net\ D}{E}\right) * (1 - \varphi)$$

And finally:

$$ROE = NOM * CT * \left(1 + \frac{net\ D}{E}\right) * (1 - \varphi)$$

We have the 3 performance indicators:

- ✓ The business performance = NOM
- ✓ The efficiency performance = ROCE
- ✓ The financial performance = ROE

We have 3 drivers:

- ✓ CT = The capital turnover linking the level of sales and the capital employed
- ✓ Net D/E = The level of net debt (sum of financial liabilities less the positive net cash position) compared to equity
- ✓ φ = The burden of the financial expenses compared to the operating profit

The Net Operating Margin (NOM), according to the level of costs (cost of goods sold and selling, general and administrative expenses) necessary to realize sales, shows the business performance.

The net operating margin is amplified or killed by the capital turnover which shows the efficiency of the financial needs to achieve the sales

At last, everything is amplified or killed by the financial structure implemented in net debt and equity mixing the level of net debt to equity and the cost of the external financing compared to the operating profit.

The net operating margin and its drivers are quotients so percentages independent from the currency used and the size of the company's numbers to facilitate comparability with other companies in the same type of business.

75 Let's analyze how to boost the efficiency performance with the capital turnover (sometimes called turbo):

A high capital turnover means to sell more with less capital employed.

In capital employed (see section 66), we have the **F**ixed **A**ssets (FA) but also the **W**orking **C**apital **R**equirement (WCR).
The WCR has to be as low as possible or even negative.
If the working capital is negative, we eliminate it from the capital employed to add it to the net debt contributing to the financial leverage seen further.
The sales managers have to be aware of the importance of the working capital requirement targeting to sell more when using the lowest working capital requirement (minimum of inventories, early collection of receivable)

76 Leverage or gearing effect

Then, we boost the financial performance thanks to the leverage effect.

Usually the leverage effect (financial leverage effect) is explained only by an amount of financial debt bigger than the level of equity.

In fact, the explanation needs more details because the leverage effect is driven by the formula:

$$\left(1 + \frac{net\ D}{E}\right) * (1 - \varphi)$$

1°) we calculate the net financial Debt.
Net Debt means that we take the financial debt less the positive net cash position. So the leverage of a high financial debt could be thwarted by a high positive net cash position.
2°) a negative WCR is also a financial debt and contributes to increase the leverage effect showing the interconnection between the operations management and the financial management.
3°) the leverage coming from the level of debt is antagonized by the cost of financing through $(1-\varphi)$
4°) φ is not an interest rate but the coverage of the net financial expenses after tax (FEXPAT) by the operating profit (NOPAT) linking the operations management and the financial management. Getting into debt is not a sin if the business performance through the NOPAT can face the cost of the financial expenses.

$$ROE = ROCE * \left(1 + \frac{net\ D}{E}\right) * (1 - \varphi)$$

We boost the financial performance (ROE) if:

$$\left(1 + \frac{net\ D}{E}\right) * (1 - \varphi) > 1$$

77 And consequently what will kill the investment performance? :

Too much cash available!!

Coming back to the concept of net Debt, if the company has a constant level of cash available bigger the financial debt, the net Debt is negative and:

$$\left(1 + \frac{net\ D}{E}\right) < 1$$

Even if in this situation φ becomes also negative so $(1-\varphi) > 1$, (because the financial revenues are higher than the financial expenses), the return on cash available is low when the interest rates are low.

So, at last:

$$\left(1 + \frac{net\ D}{E}\right) * (1 - \varphi) < 1$$

This situation will kill the efficiency performance and the business performance.

This confirms the saying that money is a means and never an end.

What are the solutions?

✓ Use the cash permanently available to invest is efficient assets which will contribute also to improve the ROCE
✓ If the company does not have any project of investment or if the level of cash is too high, decide to implement a "buy back" consisting of using the excess of cash to buy and eliminate some shares of the company. We have a win-win process: the

shareholders having decided to sell their shares to the company get money back to invest in other companies may be more profitable when the shareholders having decided to keep their shares can expect a rise of their investment thanks to a better equity leverage.

78 The responsibility

If we analyze the full responsibility of every performance, we can attribute:

- ✓ The business performance to the operations management
- ✓ The efficiency performance to the finance management
- ✓ The financial performance to the board of directors

But the chain of drivers shows a co decision:

➔ Operations /finance with the capital turnover to boost the ROCE

- ✓ Investment decision making: by reducing the amount of fixed assets and simultaneously generate more earnings
- ✓ Working capital management: by decreasing the working capital requirement
- ✓ Value creation by improving ROCE facing a constant or smaller cost of capital invested

➔ Operations/finance/board of directors with the financial leverage to boost the ROE

- ✓ Working capital management: eliminate the negative working capital requirement from the capital employed and increase the financial leverage

✓ Cost killing: reduce costs to increase the NOPAT and so φ in the financial leverage

→ Finance/board of directors with the financial leverage to boost the ROE

✓ Financial resources decision making: find the best financial debt/equity ratio
✓ Cash decision making: stick to the rule: maximize the cash flow but minimize the permanent positive net cash position

This list above is not exhaustive; you can find many other examples of shared decisions in companies.

We also only focus on the elements provided by the balance sheet and the profit and loss statement.

The cash flow statement is also important; you will discover and understand all its resources in our book:

"THE 88 essentials you must know to read and understand a cash flow statement" published by AMAZON.

The chart below summarizes the inter connection of the decision-makers in the performance improvement

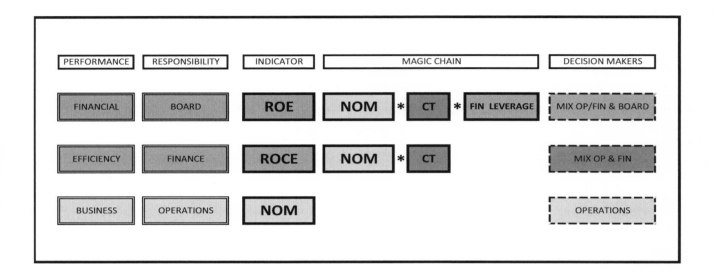

PERFORMANCE INDICATORS: TRAINING EXERCISE

79 We come back to "marvellous shoes" company.

The balance sheet at the end of the last year N – 1 was:

BALANCE SHEET as of 31/12/N-1 in 000 of $

ASSETS			LIABILITIES AND EQUITY	
CURRENT ASSETS			**SHORT TERM LIABILITIES**	
Cash and cash equivalents		148	Notes payable and bank overdrafts	290
Marketable securities			Accounts payable	109
Accounts receivable	283		Other payable	0
less allowance for doubtful accounts	0	283		
Inventories		322	**TOTAL SHORT TERM LIABILITIES**	399
Prepaid expenses		10		
			LONG TERM LIABILITIES	
TOTAL CURRENT ASSETS		763	Bonds	
			Long term bank loans	150
FIXED ASSETS				
Tangible assets	578		**TOTAL LONG TERM LIABILITIES**	150
less accumulated depreciation	229	349		
Intangible assets			**EQUITY**	
Investments		111	Capital	517
			Retained earnings	157
TOTAL FIXED ASSETS		460		
			TOTAL EQUITY	674
TOTAL ASSETS		**1 223**	**TOTAL LIABILITIES AND EQUITY**	**1 223**

We start from this situation which is the list of financial resources and needs available at the beginning of the year N.

We propose to analyze for year N the 3 performances of the company:

- ✓ The business performance
- ✓ The capital employed performance
- ✓ The invested capital performance

For that, we will build the financing system at the beginning of year N (which is the financing system at the end of year N-1) and the performing system of year N in order to calculate the Key Performance Indicators.

First of all, we build the financing system from the balance sheet.

Please refer to "The 88 essentials you must know to read and understand a balance sheet" published by AMAZON for more explanations.

5 items have to be calculated:

The financial needs and requirements (capital employed):

-The financial needs to grow in the future and develop the business: the **Fixed Assets (FA)**
-The financial requirements to run the day to day business: the **Working Capital Requirement (WCR)** already seen in section 39
The working capital requirement represents the cash missing because inventories paid are not yet sold; some earned sales are not yet collected even if some expenses are paid on credit later.

The long term financial resources (capital invested):

-The capital borrowed by the company: **Long Term Debt (LTD)**
-The capital invested by shareholders or owners: **Equity (E)**

The **Net Cash Position (Net CP)**:

- The net cash position computes the amount of cash available or invested on a short term basis and easily convertible into cash without any risk or with a slight risk minus short term financial liabilities.

This net cash position is in fact the balance between the financial long term resources raised and the financial needs requirements used by the company.

If the net cash position is positive we have a liquid asset, if the net cash position is negative we have a short term financial liability.

So the 5 items are:

FA = 460

WCR = Inventories +Accounts receivable +Prepaid expenses – Accounts payable –Other payable = 322+283+10-109= 506

LTD = 150

EQUITY = 674

Net CP = Cash – Note payable = 148-290= -142

So, the net cash position is negative and has to be posted in the resources of the system.

FINANCING SYSTEM YEAR N-1					
WCR	506	52,4%	Net CP	142	14,7%
FA	460	47,6%	LTD	150	15,5%
			EQUITY	674	69,8%
TOTAL	966	100,0%	TOTAL	966	100,0%

81 analyzing the financial system

Now, we build the common size financing system in proportion of the total of every side (966).

73

We recognize a risky system: cash shortage financing system (refer to "The 88 essentials you must know to read and understand a balance sheet")

The risk highlighted is a liquidity risk with a not stable short term financial liability (**NET CP** in red) of 15 % of the total financial resources.

Different solutions are possible:

-An operational solution: reduce the working capital requirement (**WCR**) by improving the inventories turnover even with a commercial discount, by collecting bills earlier even with a financial discount.
A better liquidity is sometimes more important than a drop of the performance.

- A financial solution: negotiate with the bankers to transform the overdraft and the short term financial liabilities into long term financial liabilities more perennial

- A strategic solution: decrease the fixed assets (**FA**) by selling non strategic assets or by negotiating a lease back for strategic assets.

The lease back could be arranged with an investment bank purchasing and paying cash a company's asset like its head office.
The company then remains there and leases it to get it back.

82 Making decisions during year N

We suppose that the board of directors, aware of the liquidity risk shown by the financing system, decides during year N to raise more financial resources than necessary to cover new financial needs:

- ✓ Invest in tangible fixed assets: 452
- ✓ Invest in the capital of their affiliate: 162
- ✓ Borrow money from the bank (Long term debt): 380
- ✓ Increase the capital of the company: 412

The total investment of 614 (452 +162) is financed by an increase of the financial resources of 792 (380 +412) from shareholders and banks generating a positive net cash of 178.

In the meantime, the company has increased its sales of 79 % from 1235 to 2211 while the net income has decreased of 19 %.

Have a look of the financial statements: profit and loss statement during year N and balance sheet at the end of year N

→ The profit and loss statement during year N:

PROFIT & LOSS STATEMENT in 000 of $	YEAR N
Net sales and services	2 211
- Cost of sales	1 599
Gross profit	612
- Selling, general and administrative expenses	402
*Earnings before interest and tax**	210
+non recurring gains	10
- Interest expenses	69
+ Financial revenues	0
Earnings before tax	151
- Income tax	60
Net Income	**91**
- Dividends	38
Addition to Retained earnings	53
*depreciation expense included 100	

You recognize the profit and loss statement proposed as a training exercise in section 54.

The depreciation expense included in the selling, general and administrative expenses is: 100

The net income of 91 is allocated as dividends for 38 and 53 as addition to retained earnings by the annual shareholders' meeting.

→ The balance sheet as of December 31st of year N:

BALANCE SHEET as of 12/31/N in 000 of $

ASSETS			LIABILITIES AND EQUITY	
CURRENT ASSETS			**SHORT TERM LIABILITIES**	
Cash and cash equivalents		90	Notes payable and bank overdrafts	290
Marketable securities			Accounts payable	94
Accounts receivable	394		Other payable	116
less allowance for doubtful accounts	0	394		
Inventories		696	**TOTAL SHORT TERM LIABILITIES**	**500**
Prepaid expenses		15		
			LONG TERM LIABILITIES	
TOTAL CURRENT ASSETS		1 195	Bonds	
			Long term bank loans	530
FIXED ASSETS				
Tangible assets	1030		**TOTAL LONG TERM LIABILITIES**	**530**
less accumulated depreciation	329	701		
Intangible assets			**EQUITY**	
Investments		273	Capital	929
			Retained earnings	210
TOTAL FIXED ASSETS		974		
			TOTAL EQUITY	**1 139**
TOTAL ASSETS		2 169	**TOTAL LIABILITIES AND EQUITY**	**2 169**

According to decisions of the board of directors:

The gross value of the tangible fixed assets is: $578 + 452 = 1030$
The financial investments are: $111 + 162 = 273$
The long term debt is: $150 + 380 = 530$
The capital is: $517 + 412 = 929$

According to the data of the profit and loss statement:

The accumulated depreciation is now: $229 + 100 = 329$
The retained earnings are: $157 + 53 = 210$

→ We can calculate now the financing system as the end of year N

FINANCING SYSTEM YEAR N					
WCR	895	47,9%	NCP	200	10,7%
FA	974	52,1%	LTD	530	28,4%
			EQUITY	1 139	60,9%
TOTAL	1 869	100,0%	TOTAL	1 869	100,0%

We can see that:

✓ The Working Capital Requirement reaches now 895 so an increase of $895 - 506 = 389$ (+77 %) linked to the increase of sales (+ 79 %)
(The WCR is, as a first approximation, proportional to sales)

✓ The amount of net fixed assets needed in the capital employed is reduced to 974 because the accumulated depreciation expense increases of 100 during year N.
The depreciation expense is a cost reducing the net income but is not a cash outflow….so it looks like a financial resource gained in addition to the income.
That's the concept of EBITDA (**E**arnings **B**efore **I**nterest, **T**ax, **D**epreciation, **A**mortization)

✓ The increase of retained earnings is like a reinvested capital so a financial resource for an amount of 53

Finally, the increase of financial requirement for 389 is financed by the positive net cash of 178 seen in section 82 (decisions of the board of directors) + 100 of depreciation expense + the addition to retained earnings of 53 for a total of: 178+100+53 = 331

So 389 – 331 = 58 of missing cash.

That's why the net cash position is still negative and reaches in the financing system now:

142 + 58 = 200

This notion of net cash position and its variance, the net cash flow, leads to another system: the cashing system which perfects the vision given by the financing system and the performing system.

We will develop in "The 88 essentials you must know to read and understand a cash flow statement" published by AMAZON.

So the financing system is still a cash shortage system with a liquidity risk even if the net cash position is reduced from 15 % to 11 %.

The next step is now to control better the working capital requirement by analyzing ratios like the turnover of inventories and the average collection period.

The comparison with other companies in the same type of industry will be a great help for operations and finance managers.

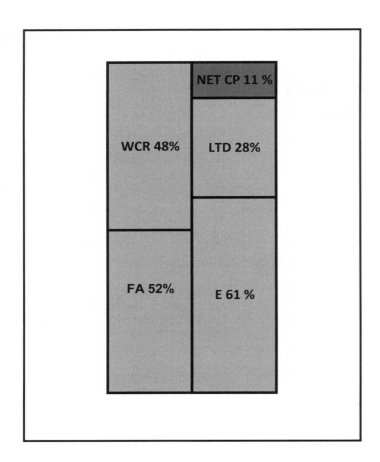

84 building the performing model

Refer to sections 55 and 56 to review the calculation of:
The gross profit, the **N**et **O**perating **P**rofit **A**fter **T**ax (NOPAT) and
the **R**ecurring *I*ncome **A**fter **T**ax (RIAT)

ROS = RIAT/SALES = 3,8 %

NOM = NOPAT/SALES = 5,7 %

GROSS MARGIN = GROSS PROFIT/SALES = 27,7 %

The total sales and services = 2 211

Gross profit = 612 => gross margin = 612/2211 = 27.7 %

NOPAT = 127 => NOM = 127/2211 = 5.7 %

RIAT = 85 => ROS = 85/2211 = 3.8 %

85 We are able now to calculate the performance indicators and first:
the business performance:

We start from the Net Operating **M**argin (NOM) = 5.7% which is
given by the performing system.

This business performance has to be analyzed over a long period like
5 years to define its trend and also compared with others competitors
in the same field of activity (bench marking).

86 then we calculate the efficiency performance

The efficiency performance indicates the return on capital employed.

The **R**eturn **O**n **C**apital **E**mployed (**ROCE**) compares the **N**et **O**perating **P**rofit **A**fter **T**ax to the financial needs and investments necessary to earn this profit which is the Capital **E**mployed (**CE**).

The **C**apital **E**mployed is the sum of the fixed assets (FA) and the positive working capital requirement (WCR).

The capital employed at the beginning of year N (according to the balance sheet at the end of year N-1 in section 80) is:

$$460 + 506 = 966$$

The NOPAT was calculated above $= 127$

$$ROCE = 127/966 = 13.1\ \%$$

<u>Pay Attention</u>: to calculate the efficiency performance of year N, we compare the items belonging to the profit and loss statement of year N with the items belonging to the balance sheet of year N-1.
The return of year N in the profit and loss statement is compared to the financial needs and investments in the balance sheet <u>available</u> at the beginning of Year N so at the end of year N-1

Some authors prefer to use the items belonging to the balance sheet of year N (so available at the end of year N) or the average value of the items in the balance sheets of year N-1 and year N.

87 At last, we compute the financial performance

The **Return On Equity (ROE)** is calculated as **Recurrent Income After Tax (RIAT)** compared to the **Equity (E)**

But we take the RIAT = 85

We compare to the equity available at the beginning of year N = 674 (Section 80)

We get:

ROE = 85/674 = 12.6 %

88 Cracking the KPI to show the magic chain

How to explain a financial performance of 12.6 % from a business performance of 5.7 %?

First, we compute the **Capital Turnover (CT)** which is the driver of the ROCE from the NO
Capital Turnover (CT) is Sales/ (Capital Employed) so:
2211/ 966 = 2.29
It means that every dollar of capital employed is used to generate 2.29 dollars of sales.

It is very important again to analyze this driver in the light of the trend over 5 years and by comparison with other companies in the same type of business.

We double check:
ROCE = NOM * CT
13.1 % = 5.7 % * 2.29 (rounded figures)

Then, we calculate the leverage effect with the 2 factors:

➜ The level of net financial debt over equity
➜ The cost of financing

The net financial debt is the balance between the long term financial debt and the positive cash position at the beginning of year N
Here we have a negative net cash position so the net financial debt is the sum of the long term financial debt (150) and the negative net cash position which is a short term financial liability (142).

The net debt is: $150 + 142 = 292$

As equity = 674 at the same date, the leverage of the net debt is:

$1 + \text{net debt/equity} = 1 + 292/674 = 1.43$

But this leverage is impacted by the cost of financing through $(1 - \varphi)$

With $\varphi = \text{NFEXPAT} / \text{NOPAT}$ for year N (figures are in section55)

So $\varphi = 42/127 = 0.33$
$1 - \varphi = 0.67$

The final leverage (sometimes called equity multiplier) is the leverage of net debt * impact of cost financing $= 1.43 * 0.67 \approx 0.96$

We double check:

$\text{ROE} = \text{ROCE} * (1 + \text{net debt/equity}) * (1 - \varphi)$

$12.6\% = 13.1\% * 0.96$ (rounded figures)

We notice that the financial performance is killed by the equity multiplier (0.96) because of the level of the cost of financing compared to the operating profit.

During year N, (according to the financing system end of year N), The leverage will move from 1.43 to $1 + (530+200)/1139 = 1.64$ So the killing effect of the equity multiplier for 0.96 will be transform into a gearing effect of $1.64 * 0.67 = 1.10$ if the impact of the cost of financing $(1 - \varphi)$ remains constant during year N+1

The drivers of the performance indicators are summarized in the chart below:

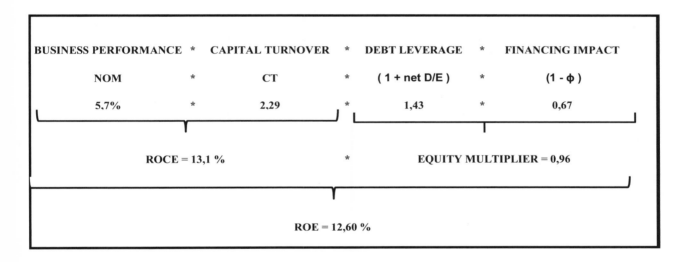

The figures given by the past financial statements are important to calculate and check the drivers and so to implement the algorithms necessary to build the systems (financing, performing and cashing systems)

Then, the systems are very useful during the budget process to forecast the consequences of business development hypotheses and to validate operations and financial decisions.

I hope you have enjoyed our explanations about the profit and loss statement's secrets.

I remind you some books useful to understand other aspects of financial accounting and corporate finance.

"The 88 essentials a MBA student must know in financial accounting"

"The 88 essentials you must know to read and understand a balance sheet"

Published by AMAZON in hard copy or Kindle format

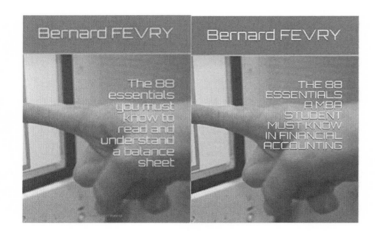

Coming soon:

"The 88 essentials you must know to read and understand a cash flow statement"
 "The 88 essentials an entrepreneur must know in accounting and in finance to run a business"

Thank you to stay tuned with our website:
www.mycampusfinance.com

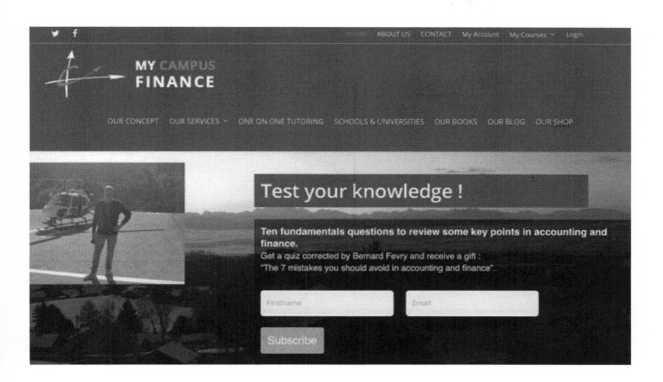

Test your knowledge !

Ten fundamentals questions to review some key points in accounting and finance.

Get a quiz corrected by Bernard Fevry and receive a gift :
"The 7 mistakes you should avoid in accounting and finance".

Firstname | Email

Subscribe

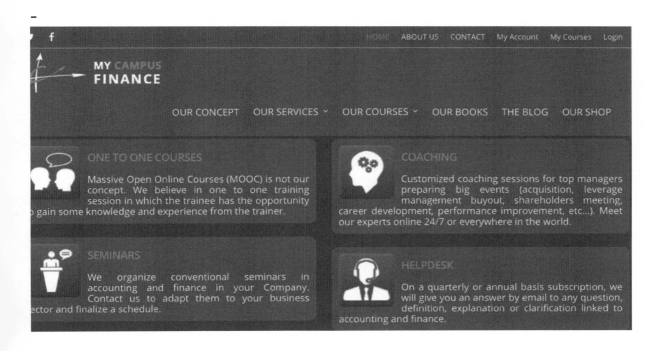

ONE TO ONE COURSES

Massive Open Online Courses (MOOC) is not our concept. We believe in one to one training session in which the trainee has the opportunity to gain some knowledge and experience from the trainer.

COACHING

Customized coaching sessions for top managers preparing big events (acquisition, leverage management buyout, shareholders meeting, career development, performance improvement, etc...). Meet our experts online 24/7 or everywhere in the world.

SEMINARS

We organize conventional seminars in accounting and finance in your Company. Contact us to adapt them to your business sector and finalize a schedule.

HELPDESK

On a quarterly or annual basis subscription, we will give you an answer by email to any question, definition, explanation or clarification linked to accounting and finance.

Bernard Fevry

Bernard FEVRY is a French Certified Public Accountant, Legal Auditor and EMBA INSEAD. After an experience as financial manager in a Swiss pharmaceutical company, he runs an auditing agency in France and a financial consultancy company in Switzerland.

He taught as a lecturer at HEC PARIS School of Management and ESCP Europe, his main topics are the financial accounting, the corporate finance, the financial markets and the Islamic finance in MBA et EMBA programs. He conducts also intra-companies seminars in corporate finance, value creation and financial modeling analysis for international groups. He is the writer of many books and articles.

Stay tuned with the lastest news of MyCampusFinance.com

Videos, Advices, News, Tutorials, Seminars...

f 🐦

| Firstname | Email | Subscribe |

Made in the USA
Monee, IL
28 June 2022

98768034R00053